M

Succ

Mindpower 1

Succeed
at School

J. H. Brennan

An Armada Original

Succeed at School was first published in Armada in 1990

Armada is an imprint of the Children's Division,
part of the Collins Publishing Group,
8 Grafton Street, London W1X 3LA

© 1990 J. H. Brennan

Printed and bound in Great Britain by
William Collins Sons & Co.Ltd, Glasgow

CONTENTS

YOU Can Beat
the Exam System

Imagine this:

It's exam day. Everybody round you is falling apart with nerves. Rumours are flying that it's the hardest paper ever. Even the brainboxes are going down like flies. And anyone who fails gets hanged.

This is not good news for you. You've had trouble with the subject all your life. You didn't work hard during term. And there was a disco on the night you planned to do your revision.

All the same, you stroll into the exam hall cool as Superdude, tip your hat to the examiner, flick a speck of dust off your immaculate sleeve and slide the paper into your line of vision with a small, mysterious smile.

Long before the time is up, while everybody else is struggling, you snap the cap back on your pen, tip your hat to the examiner again, and stroll out into the sunshine in search of a gourmet plate of fish and chips.

And when the results come through, you've topped the class! You've powered your way through the exam with almost no effort at all and still scored better than you ever did before!

If that sounds like a fairy tale, read on — I have good news for you.

The fact is, nearly every exam you'll ever have to sit is a test of memory. History.. Geography ... Literature ... French ... German ... Latin ... Chemistry ... Physics ... Fill out the list for yourself. Teachers like to think they're testing your understanding . But they're not. A chimp with a photographic memory could get a pass in any of these subjects — and top marks in most of them.

Even with subjects like Maths or Geometry, where you really are demolished if you don't have a proper understanding, a good memory will boost your marks, maybe make the difference between success and failure. The trouble is, you don't have a good memory — right? Wrong. What you don't have is a trained memory.

This is pretty odd when you stop to think about it. If

you go to a school where 75%, 80% of subjects taught need you to remember stuff, you'd think somebody would have had the sense to put Memory Training down on the curriculum. No way.

But by the time you finish this book, you will have a trained memory. Getting that way will take a little bit of your time, but not much. It will require a little bit of effort, but not much. Most of it should even be a lot of fun.

And when you're finished, you will be able to remember anything you want to. Dates, places, lists, names, formulae, who unified Germany, the basic relationship between Energy and Mass — whatever.

Let me be specific. Here, as a promise, are a few of the things you will be able to do if you're willing to work your way through this book.

* You will be able to read through a random list of twenty, fifty, one hundred or more items, then repeat them back, without error, forwards and backwards.

* You will be able to remember instantly the fifth item on the list ... or the thirty-third, or the eighty-ninth.

* You will be able to burn facts, figures dates and
  places into your head so indelibly that you will still
  be able to remember them weeks, months, even years
  later.

You will be able to remember names and match them
instantly. You will be able to study more effectively —
which means studying with less effort for better results.
When the techniques you'll learn become instinctive, so
you start to apply them without thinking, you will find
your problem is forgetting something, not remembering
it.

And that's going to let you smash your way through
most of your examinations just as you imagined
yourself doing a couple of minutes ago. Not all your
exams: most.

But most will be enough.

The Five-Minute Fun Test That Proves You Too Can Have a Super Memory

Let me show you how easy and effective mindpower training really is. In fact, let me prove it to you. Here's a list for you to remember:

Typewriter
Snake
Washing machine
Teddy bear
Bronze statue
Cactus
Painting
Egyptian mummy
Persian rug
Egg-cup
Dictionary
Can of Coca-Cola
Telephone
Horse
Notebook
Ship in a bottle

Walking stick
Plate of egg and chips
Elephant
Potted palm
Guitar
Pair of boots
Motor car
Vampire bat
Pound of butter

That could be a shopping list your mum made out. (If it wasn't for the vampire bat.) Or it could be a list of chemical components in a particular compound. Or the names of British Cabinet members in 1892. What you're dealing with in detail doesn't matter: it's the principle that counts.

There are twenty-five random items on the list I gave and it's your job to remember what they are.

Has your blood run cold? Don't worry — you'll remember them easily once you know how. But first, I want you to try to remember them the old way. The old way is to read that list over and over until you think it's more or less stuck. Typewriter ... snake ... washing machine ... teddy bear ... over and over until the whole list sticks, or until you get bored out of your tree, whichever is the sooner.

Take up to ten minutes to learn the list by heart the old way. Once you have learned the list by heart, or think you have learned the list by heart, or are so exhausted by trying to learn the list by heart that you just don't care any more, I want you to go off and do something interesting for half an hour.

That's right, I want you to tear yourself away from this book and go off and do something else.

After a fun half hour or so — it needn't be exact — come back and write down as many items from that list as you can remember. Don't worry about the order or anything like that. Just write down as many as you can remember. When you've finished, check what you've written against the original list and give yourself one mark for each item correctly remembered.

Not very good, was it?But however low you scored, you can take consolation in the fact that most people — kids or adults — wouldn't do any better. A lot of them would do a lot worse. Without a trained memory, half a dozen correct is about as good as you're likely to get.

But rest easy. You were doing it the hard way. Now let's do it the easy way ... and the better way.

Imagine your own home. By 'imagine' I mean make a picture in your mind. Visualise your home the way you might do if you were daydreaming. For the next few minutes, your home is going to be your locus, the place where you put things you want to remember.

Imagine yourself standing outside your own front door. Try to visualise it as vividly as possible, noting the colour of the paint, the shine on the brass knocker and so on. I don't know what your home looks like, of course, so I'll use a locus of my own as a demonstration of what you should do in order to memorise your list. You simply substitute the features in your own home and do as I do.

Okay, I'm imagining myself standing outside the front door of my own home. There's a flight of three stone steps going up to the door. On those steps I imagine a typewriter (the first item on the list.) I imagine it's a really big typewriter so I have to climb over it awkwardly to get to the door.

Having climbed over the typewriter and reached the

front door, I open it up and step into my front hall. To my absolute horror, there is a massive snake (item 2 on the list) rearing up on the mat inside, poised to strike.

Leaping nimbly aside, because I can still do things like that in my head, I avoid the snake and glance around. There is a door on my right which leads into a living room and a staircase directly ahead. I ignore the staircase and turn right into my living room.

In the middle of my brand new green carpet (bought only three weeks ago at considerable personal expense) is a washing machine, the third item on the list. Worse, some idiot has switched it on and put in too much detergent so that it is belching foam all over the carpet and the furniture.

I deal with this crisis by ignoring it and leave the living room through the door in the left hand wall which leads into my dining room. Sitting at the head of my polished mahogany dining table, busily eating porridge, is a life-size teddy bear which has broken out in pink spots.

Sitting opposite the teddy bear is a bronze statue of a horse, its bottom bulging out over the chair and threatening to break it completely. The bronze statue of the horse is drinking a cup of tea.

Getting the hang of it? As you move through your home locus, what you have to do is imagine the various items on your list in the different places you pass through.

Don't waste a lot of time on any one: just visualise as clearly as you can, put the item in place, then imagine yourself going on to the next room, corridor of whatever. As you can see from the example, you can put two or more items in the same room if you think you might be running out of space.

A few tips (which we will come back to later) ...

* Exaggerate the size of the item, unless it happens to be pretty big to begin with. When I started out, for instance, I imagined a really massive typewriter on the front steps.

* Make your mental picture dramatic if the situation permits. It was a pretty dramatic situation for me to walk into my living room and find foam all over the place from that stupid washing machine.

* Make some, all or most of your mental pictures

ludicrous or amusing or silly.

Go all the way through your home and all the way through your list until you have placed all twenty-five items, finishing with the pound of butter.

Now comes the moment of truth. Put the list away, take a pen and paper, imagine yourself at the front door of your house and write down 'typewriter', since that is what you can see on the front steps. Climb over the typewriter, open the front door, leap aside nimbly as the cobra strikes at you, then write down 'snake'.

Take the same route through your home as you did before and write down the various items as you find them in the rooms you visit.

Don't worry if you draw an occasional blank. This is the first time you've tried the technique and nobody expects perfection. Just keep going to the next room and write down what you find there. When you've finished, check your score.

You may actually have all twenty-five items correct (and in the correct order as well) but even if you have not, I know you will have done better — far better —

using this simple visualisation technique than you did trying to learn the items off by heart the old way. Furthermore, I know you will have found it a whole lot easier. Of course you cheated a little. The first time you didn't try to remember your list until you'd gone off and amused yourself for half an hour. This time you started to write it down straight away.

But let's find out how well you really remember that list. Forget half an hour. Tomorrow sometime, or the day after, visualise yourself walking through your home and write down the various items you have placed there starting with the typewriter and ending with the pound of butter. I guarantee you will still remember all or most of them.

What you have in that simple little exercise in mindpower is absolute proof your memory can be improved quickly, easily, enjoyably. (Didn't you have fun with the Egyptian mummy?) By the time you have finished this book, if you're prepared to work at the system, you will have a super power memory.

And with a super power memory, you will have very little problem beating the education system.

Woolgathering Your
Way to Mindpower

The locus is the oldest mindpower memory technique still in common use. But it isn't the most useful or the best. It's great if you have a list of things you want to remember, like the list I gave you as a test, and it does let you impress people by reciting a long catalogue of items forwards or backwards (just reverse the route you take through your home.)

But it won't help you remember names, for example, or recollect abstractions or let you call out instantly the one hundred and seventy-third thing you have just memorised. In other words, its use is limited.

That's not to say you should ignore the locus. It's the five-finger exercise of mindpower because it introduces the most fundamental mindpower principle there is:

You can work miracles if you are prepared to visualise.

Throughout the rest of this book, I'll be showing you the remarkable things visualisation can do for your memory. Just about every memory technique I know is based on visualisation or has visualisation coming into it somewhere.

If you can daydream, you can visualise. And if you can visualise, you can remember.

Of course, visualisation involves more than seeing pictures in your mind. As an experienced day-dreamer, you should be able to imagine sounds as well. You might even be able to imagine textures, tastes and smells. The better you can do so, the more powerful your mind will eventually become.

Which brings me to a second principle of mindpower:

Young minds are almost always far more powerful than old minds.

Old minds know more, but young minds can do more. The only thing is, they have to be shown how. Most times they aren't, so all that potential rots on the vine.

Let's stop yours rotting straight away with a lightning training course in memory.

A Twelve-Word Lesson
in the Awesome Art of Memory

Harry Lorayne has the most phenomenal memory in the world. He makes a living out of demonstrating how phenomenal it is. For example:

When he isn't touring with his stage show or appearing on television, Harry gets a lot of invitations to talk about memory to various organisations. He is very much in demand as an after-dinner speaker. He gives a lot of talks at Rotary Club luncheons.

Before the Rotary Club lunch starts, Harry stands at the door along with the Club President and is introduced to every Rotarian coming in. In America, where Harry Lorayne lives, Rotary Clubs can get very big. Some of them have a membership of a thousand, fifteen hundred or more. So there are days when Harry gets introduced to upwards of one thousand five hundred people. That's one thousand five hundred brand new names and faces. When everybody is in their place, they have lunch. After lunch, which takes about an hour to an hour and a half, Harry stands up and talks for twenty minutes on the subject of memory. When he's finished, he asks for questions ... and makes a promise.

The promise is that if he can't greet the questioner by name, he will pay him $1,000.

In all the years he has been making that promise, Harry Lorayne has never had to pay out a cent.

So what has Harry Lorayne got to say about the art of memory? Harry Lorayne says that most people don't forget — they just never take the trouble to remember in the first place.

Most people don't forget — they just never take the trouble to remember. That's worth thinking about, just for a minute.

You're at a party and you've just been introduced to the new kid on the block. Five minutes later you can't remember her name. But it's not that you've forgotten. It's just that you didn't make the slightest effort to remember when you were being introduced.

Without flicking back, you might be hard put to recall the title on the first section of this book. You read it all right, maybe not so very long ago, but you've forgotten it now because you didn't make an effort to remember.

Most people don't forget — they just never take the trouble to remember.

That's your first lesson. Remembering requires effort. But the effort has to come when you're filing away something in your memory banks, not when you're trying to recall it later. I'll give you that again:

The effort has to come when you're filing away something in your memory banks, not when you're trying to recall it later.

That's just the opposite of the way most people do it. It's probably the opposite of the way you've been doing it all your life. If so, it's the first thing you have to change.

The techniques in this book are all about ways of filing away things you want to remember. Get that right and recall is no trouble at all. But you have to make the effort in the first place. No system works if you can't be bothered to apply it.

Announcing:
The New Improved
(And Very Personal)
Memory Locus!

The locus I suggested at the start of this book was your own home. The locus I want you to use now is you, specifically your body. It's an up-to-date, wholly portable locus you can use like a mental Filofax to make sure you remember everything you have to do today.

Your body is something you carry around with you all the time which makes it the perfect small-scale locus. Here's how to use it:

Let's assume you have a shortish list you want to memorise. Only this time, instead of confining yourself to objects (as we did in the first list) try mixing in a few actions — things you have to do.

Your short list might go something like this:

1. A telephone.
2. Buy a cone of ice-cream (with strawberry

topping.)

3. Fix the vacuum cleaner.
4. A paperback book.
5. A statue of a frog.
6. Find out what's showing at the Odeon.
7. De-flea the dog.
8. Jar of mixed pickles.
9. Bag of crisps.
10. Walking stick.
11. Elastic band.
12. Top hat.
13. Child's doll.
14. Post letter to uncle.
15. Pair of scissors.

That's a much more difficult list to remember than the first one you tried. Not because it's longer (actually it's shorter) but because it goes beyond simple objects and moves into things you have to do.

You'd wonder how you are going to slot stuff like that into a locus, even a new, improved locus like the one we'll be working with in a minute. But hang in there, all will be revealed.

Your body locus works like this:

a) Imagine the first item on your list (the telephone in this instance) as a very peculiar hat which perches on the top of your head.

b) Imagine the next item on your list pasted onto your forehead.

c) Visualise the third item on your list as pictured in a neon sign which flashes on and off out of your eyes.

Getting the idea? Now work your way down your body storing items from your list in the following way.

Item 4 is stuffed up your nose. (Yes, I know it's revolting, but you'll remember it.)

Item 5 goes into your mouth which has now become a tunnel.

Item 6 is balanced on your chin as if you were a juggler.

Item 7 can be clearly seen inside your throat, which has now become a transparent cylinder.

Item 8 is strapped to your right arm so you can hardly lift it.

Item 9 has actually become your left arm, giving you a truly monstrous look.

Item 10 has been dropped into your chest where it is kept in a rubber sack the shape of your lungs.

Item 11 (you're going to like this) is tied to your belly-button with a big pink bow.

Item 12 is slung low over your hips from a belt so that it flaps and bounces like a Western hero's six-shooter.

Item 13 has transformed itself into two and each copy is sticking out of the inside of your thighs making it extremely difficult for you to walk.

Item 14 is now pasted to your knees, making you wonder what it would be like if you had to kneel down. Item 15 is under your feet and since in this instance it's a pair of scissors, you'd better watch out you don't cut yourself.

Use your body locus exactly the same way you used

your home locus. Visualise the item you want to remember in or on a particular part of your body. Always do this in the same sequence, starting with the top of your head, moving down to your forehead and following on in the same order as I listed above:

1   Top of the head
2   Forehead
3   Eyes
4   Nose
5   Mouth
6   Chin
7   Throat
8   Right arm
9   Left arm
10 Chest
11 Belly-button
12 Hips
13 Inside thighs
14 Knees
15 Feet

Don't waste time concentrating or trying to remember. But try to see the placement clearly in your mind's eye.

You'll have noticed in my example several parts of your

body were actually transformed into something else — your mouth into a tunnel, your throat into a transparent tube and so on. You can make the same sort of transformation in other body parts if you wish; and if you find it helps.

Furthermore, the trick you learned in your home locus of making remembered items bigger or more dramatic or just plain silly works well in your body locus too. In every instance try to get size, number, drama or silliness into your visualisation. If there's a phone on top of your head, make it a huge phone, so you're bowed down under the weight. If there's a statue of a frog in your mouth, make it rush in or out of that tunnel like an express train.

So far, of course, I've been avoiding the tricky area. I've been pretending the current list is just like the first one — all solid objects. But it isn't. Throughout that list there are actions, things you want to remember to do. How do you work them in?
Let's look a bit more closely at those actions. As extracted from your list, they are as follows:

1. Buy a cone of ice-cream (with strawberry topping.)

2. Fix the vacuum cleaner.
3. Find out what's showing at the Odeon.
4. De-flea the dog.
5. Post letter to uncle.

The interesting thing about all five of those actions is that each one involves a thing. Some of them involve two things. You have:

a) An ice-cream cone
b) A vacuum cleaner
c) The Odeon cinema
d) Your dog and his fleas
e) A letter and your uncle

Once you start to think about actions you have to take, you will very quickly find they almost always involve one or more things somewhere along the line. And nine times out of ten, if you remember the things you will automatically remember the action you wanted to take concerning them.

So all you have to do is paste the ice-cream cone on your forehead and you're reminded you have to buy one, flash the neon vacuum cleaner out of your eyes and you'll recollect you have to fix it. And so on.

But suppose, just suppose, you manage to hit up against one of those rare situations where remembering the thing actually doesn't help you recall the action?

Simple — you visualise yourself carrying out the action and paste that whole mental movie onto the relevant bit of your body.

How Making
Daisy-Chains Can
Fill Your Head With Facts

By now, you've learned another valuable lesson about memory:

If you can't remember something, peg it to something else that you can.

So far you've pegged items onto rooms in your home and bits of your body. Your next step is to peg them onto one another. That way you can forget all about loci and concentrate on filing memories in such a way that each one actually helps you remember another.

With this technique, you've moving towards the way your mind naturally stores memories. It's not very logical, not very rational. There are no neat pigeonholes labelled A, B and C. Instead, your mind associates a whole heap of disconnected stuff and drops it into a bottomless bin. Here's an illustration of the way it works:

One day you're out for a walk in the country. You're

looking at a sheep in a field when a red sports car, driven too fast, careers around the corner, blasts its horn and zips so close you have to leap aside to avoid getting knocked down.

While this mess is going on, your mind is busy filing away memories. These memories include the sheep in the field, the smell of honeysuckle in the hedgerow, the colour of the car that nearly killed you and the particular sound of its two-tone horn.

Normally, your mind would hardly bother filing these memories away at all — individually, none of them are all that impressive. But in this instance, because you were scared out of your skin, everything in the dramatic scene is filed, and everything is automatically associated with everything else.

What this means is that from then on, any one of the memories — the particular sound of a car horn, for example — will tend to recall the whole scene. Which is fair enough, except that given enough time, the whole scene recedes so far into the past that it is no longer recalled as an entity. But the associations are still there, because that's the way your mind filed them.
And because the associations are still there, sheep will

tend to make you see red (the colour of the car) which will in turn remind you of the smell of honeysuckle, which curiously recalls the sound of a car horn. What you have, in other words, is a daisy-chain of linked ideas which make no sense whatsoever unless you know the circumstances that linked them.

You can examine a few of these daisy-chains for yourself by putting a couple of your friends through what's called a word association test. Ask them to tell you the first word that comes into their head when you say the word Mother. Then feed back the word they give you with the same instruction. In a couple of minutes, you'll have a whole long daisy-chain to look at.

But even though you start with exactly the same word, you'll get a totally different daisy-chain from everybody you try this one on. That's because everybody forms their associations in different circumstances.

But if the circumstances differ, the method of association is exactly the same for everybody. And once you know the trick, you can use it to form associations of your own, to make your own daisy-chains at a conscious level.

When you have made your own daisy-chain, all you really have to remember is the first link. Because the first link is all you need to drag the whole chain out.

This system is called (oddly enough) the Link System of Memory and you will be delighted to hear you already know the principle ways to make it work.

Let's recap for a minute. When we were dealing with the locus method, it turned out that the best way to get something into your memory banks was to visualise. For some reason, pictures in the head were far easier to remember than words.

The next thing we found was that if you visualised BIG or turned a single item into a whole heap of the same item, remembering was easier still.

And finally we found that if you made the picture dramatic, or, better yet, silly, remembering was easiest of all.

All this is still part of the link method. Here comes another list so you can try it out:

Mountain
Fish
Oil painting
Chair
Apple
Can of Baked Beans
Dragon
Hammer
Spectacles
Kite
Skeleton
Earphones
Bed
Carpet
Notebook

Fifteen items. For simplicity, I've kept them all things rather than actions, but you know how to deal with actions now and the action remembering techniques that work with a locus will work just as well with the Link Method.

To form those fifteen items into a daisy-chain, you start with the first item on the list, which was mountain.

As you already know, it's no good filing away the word

'mountain' — words are hard to remember. What you have to do is file away a mental picture of a mountain. The exact mental picture is up to you.

There's no need to spend a lot of time on your visualisation. All you need is a quick, clear mental picture of a mountain. Hold it in your mind for a second, then go on to the next stage.

The next stage is linking your picture of a mountain (which you now remember) with item 2 on the list. Item 2 on the list is a fish. And the link you make in your mind between mountain and fish must be dramatic, exaggerated and, above all, ridiculous. That last one is really important. The day you get the hang of creating ridiculous associations is the day you build yourself a memory that will astonish your friends and help you smash your way through examinations.

What sort of association can you make? You might visualise a mountain of fish, a huge heap of fish as high as Everest. As a link, it has something going for it — it's exaggerated. But it's not exactly ridiculous, so you should be able to do better.

How about a mountain swimming through the ocean? That's a lot more ridiculous and consequently a lot better. Or how about a mountain with a fisherman's hook dangling over it and the mountain rising up to take the bait?

While my example associations will work okay, they won't work half as well as ridiculous links you create for yourself. This is because we're working with your head, your mind, your memory and you know better than anybody what strikes you as funny or ridiculous.

We're talking creativity here and I want you to give it your best shot ... and keep on giving it your best shot until forming ridiculous associations between items you want to remember becomes second nature to you.

Once you've dreamed up a ridiculous association between mountain and fish you have to create a link between fish and oil painting. Try that now.

Maybe the first thing that came into your head was a painting of a fish. That's okay — sometimes I get lazy too. But a painting of a fish just isn't a ridiculous association, so you're going to have to do better. How about a fish that's sitting up in a high-backed chair, posing to have its portrait painted? That's a pretty ridiculous association and one that will work for me.

But the ridiculous link you make for yourself will work better.

Okay, now you've got a mountain that reminds you of a fish and a fish that reminds you of an oil painting. Your daisy-chain has got three links already.

For the next link, you need to find a ridiculous association between an oil painting and a chair. You will notice at this point that I am not asking you to associate chair with mountain or fish. You have already made those links in your daisy-chain, so you can afford to forget them ... until, of course, you want to remember them.

Maybe the way to go is to imagine yourself walking into a friend's house and sitting down on an extremely valuable oil painting. Not very ridiculous, but at least you could add a bit of drama by having your bum go right through it so that you fall on your back on the f.oor with your legs up in the air.

That's not a ridiculous image, but it is dramatic, so maybe it will do. Of course, if the painting was a painting of a chair and you were so dim you tried to sit in the chair in the painting and that's how you broke the painting, then you might think that was ridiculous. But don't waste time on my associations. The ridiculous links you forge yourself will always work better.

The existing links in your daisy-chain — mountain, fish, oil painting, chair — are all items you now remember. (Take my word for it at the moment: later you can check it out for yourself.) And in every case, you made the link by pegging the new thing — the item to be remembered — onto the thing you already remembered.

You started by remembering mountain, then you pegged fish onto that. So now you remembered fish, you pegged oil painting onto fish, then pegged chair onto oil painting.

Remember the principle I quoted: If you can't remember something, peg it to something you can.

Now you have remembered chair, you have to peg the next thing on the list, which is apple. This is no different from the rest. Make a ridiculous association between chair and apple. You sat on an oil painting instead of a chair, maybe you could try biting on a chair instead of an apple.

I really don't want to give you any more of my associations. As I keep saying, you should be creating your own. It's your head, your mind, your memory and your daisy-chain. Make it yourself and it will work. Copy my examples and it won't work so well.

But if I can't make the links for you, I can at least let you have the basic principles of making a successful link:

Principle 1:

Make it big. Make it exaggerated. Get it out of proportion. When you broke the painting in that earlier example, you should have visualised yourself smashing it into pieces, cracking the floor, crashing through the wall, bringing down the roof.

Principle 2:

Make it active. I've already told you that when you want to remember an action rather than a thing, you can run a mental movie in your head. But the fact is, you can always remember a thing better by having it star in an action movie anyway. Movement is good, action is better and violent action is best.

Principle 3:

Play the numbers game as multiples will be remembered better than singles. If you're trying to remember the skeleton on your list, don't just visualise a link with one skeleton — wheel in a dozen, or a hundred, or a thousand.

Principle 4:

Use substitution. This is perhaps the most obvious principle. When I was linking apple with chair a minute ago, I suggested you were biting on a chair the way you might bite on an apple. In other words, I was suggesting you substitute one for the other.

So now you know how it's done. Start with mountain and make your own daisy-chain which takes in every item on the list, all the way through to notebook at the end. Make your associations as ridiculous as possible and, most important of all, see them in your mind's eye, even if only for a moment.

When you have gone through the whole list, turning it into a mental daisy-chain, test yourself on how well you remembered. Once again you may not be absolutely perfect on your first attempt, but you should do at least as well as you did the first time you used a locus.

Furthermore, you will find it very useful to examine those few items on the list that you couldn't remember. What associations did you use? Chances are they weren't ridiculous enough, or exaggerated enough, or big enough. Improve your associations and try again until you have the entire list in your head. And just like the locus system, you will find it stays there. Hours, days, even weeks later, all you need do is remember the first item on the list and you can haul in the entire daisy-chain.

But suppose you forget the first item on the list ...?

You can always put one more link into your daisy-chain and associate the first item with a place, person or circumstance you plan to meet up with when you need to remember the list.

Why You Remember
Why You Don't

Test yourself. Take a brief glance at the next two lines.

AN INEXPENSIVE HOME COMPUTER

76-45872955473-7814-63259814

Now turn the book over, take a pencil and paper and write down those two lines from memory, one below the other.

The question is, which did you find easier to remember?

It's no real contest, is it? Even without loci or daisy chains, the first line was pretty easy. The second line you probably found just about impossible.

Yet both those lines contained exactly the same number of symbols — twenty-five. In the first line you had twenty-five letters of the alphabet. In the second you had twenty-five numbers. So how come you found the first line so easy while the second line was so hard?

The answer is, the first line had meaning. The letters of the alphabet were arranged to form words and the words painted a familiar picture. The second line had no meaning at all. It was just a string of random numbers with a few dashes scattered to break them up a bit.

Here's another test. Read the following passage very carefully:

You are driving a train running between the suburbs and the city which starts its journey with one hundred passengers.

At its first stop, three passengers get off and twenty-three new passengers get on.

The train travels another mile to the next station where ten people get off, but only five get on.

At each of the next three stops, ten people get off and five get on.

By now the train is approaching the heart of the city so that at the next stop twenty people get off and ten get on.

While still some distance from its destination, jammed points divert the train into a siding where it is forced to halt for seventeen minutes.

Towards the end of that time, ten passengers become impatient and leave the train to walk.

But the points are fixed and the train continues on its way with one more stop before reaching its destination.

At this stop, one hundred passengers get off and ten get on.

Once again, there are two questions, which you should try to answer without rereading the paragraph. The first is, how many people were left on the train when it reached its final destination? The second is, how many stops did the train make?

There's a third question: which of the first two questions did you find easier to answer?

I may be wrong, but my feeling is you made a reasonable stab at question 1, but found question 2 very difficult indeed. The reason why I think this is that the whole test was structured so you would conclude the number of people on the train was important. This made you take an interest in the numbers getting on and getting off. Chances are, since you knew it was a test, you were counting in your head as you went along.

But there was nothing to suggest the number of stops was important, so chances are you didn't bother to count those. Hence you had an answer to the first question and not the second.

Either way, the key to remembering was exactly the same. If you took an interest you tended to remember. If you didn't take an interest, you forgot.

Let me underline that point with one more question. What was the name of the train driver? Without checking back, take a pen or pencil and write it in

the space below.

_____

Not so easy, was it? Even if you figured I might ask the number of stops, it's unlikely you would have expected a question about the driver. So you didn't pay attention; and because you didn't pay attention, you forgot who was behind the wheel, or whatever they use to steer a train.

If you haven't checked, you may even have convinced yourself this was a trick question and the paragraph didn't actually tell you who the driver was. In a way you're right and in a way you're wrong. It was a trick question. The paragraph didn't actually name the driver, but it did tell you who the driver was.

Read the first five words of the paragraph again. They state quite clearly that the train driver was you. The name you should have written in the space above was your own.

Meaning and interest ... two reasons why you tend to remember. Here's a third reason — and a third test.

Have a look at this mini poster:

HE WHO
HESITATES IS
IS LOST!

Now turn the book over and write down what it says on the poster. (You needn't draw a box around it unless you want to.) Don't read on until you've done so.

Did you remember to write down the X at the end? Of course you did! But did you also remember to put in the extra 'is'? That poster doesn't read 'He who hesitates is lost!' It actually reads, 'He who hesitates is is lost!'

If you noticed the extra word in the familiar saying, you really should congratulate yourself. Very few people do. (Test the poster on a group of your friends — you'll soon find you can fool a lot of them.)

The fact is, few people are particularly observant. They look at things but don't really pay attention, don't really see them. This is especially true when they are looking at something familiar.

So even though you saw the poster, even though you read the poster, chances are you didn't really remember the poster. Because meaning isn't enough and interest isn't enough. To remember, you also need observation and attention.

How to Remember Numbers

By the time you are fully grown, your brain will have the capacity to remember $2^{10,000,000,000}$ bits of information.

That's a lot of memory — more than enough to remember absolutely everything you ever see, hear, taste, touch and smell throughout your life, with lots left over for your memories of heaven afterwards.

So you've got more than enough capacity for tricky stuff like memorising numbers. Yet for most people, anything longer than three or four digits is out of the question. This is because most numbers have no meaning and for most people very little interest.

Let's go back to that test you did earlier, the two-liner with the inexpensive home computer. The second line of that test — the one you had problems remembering — was:

76-45872955473-7814-63259814

Take out the dashes, which are only in for show, and you have 7645872955473781463259814. If I were to tell you that your life depended on memorising that entire number within the next five minutes, you might start to feel just a little bit nervous.

All the same, although your life doesn't depend on it, you should be able to memorise that — or any other twenty-five digit number — well within the five minute limit, once you know how.

This memory feat does, however, require you to do some very important preparation.

Professor A.C. Aitken of Edinburgh University could recite the value of pi to 1000 decimal places. Amazing though this might sound, it did not actually involve his memorising a thousand different numbers. The actual number symbols he had to recall was only ten — 0, 1, 2, 3, 4, 5, 6, 7, 8, 9. His real problem was getting them in the right order.

The fundamental difficulty in remembering numbers lies with those ten digits. Unlike the letters of the alphabet, they do not convey specific meanings when you combine them. And as things in themselves, one is very much like the other.

Now you can go some way towards memorising numbers by placing gigantic cut-out versions of them in your locus. You can try that out right now using the first half dozen digits of the number 76458729554737781463259814 for practice.

Leave the giant 7 propped up against your front door, the 6 lying on the floor in the hall, the 4 on the table in the dining room ... and so on. You might be interested to find out exactly how many numbers you can actually memorise in this way. Certainly you will do better using a locus than simply concentrating, but however well you do, the method is still not as efficient as it might be. And if you try the daisy-chain method with numbers, the whole system is likely to fall apart before you even start.

The big difficulty, as you've now doubtless discovered for yourself, is that visualising single digits is no fun. Apart from making them big, there's not much you can do with them. Put plainly, numbers are a bore.

But cast your mind back to that memory rule you learned: If you can't remember something, peg it to something else you can.

That's what you have to do with the ten digits which go to make up every number you will ever use.

There are a couple of ways you can do this. Try them both and use whichever comes easier and works best for you.

The first is derived from that old children's rhyme, the one that starts:

One, two .... buckle my shoe
Three, four ... knock at the door
Five, six ... pick up sticks

And so on ...

That little rhyme gives you immediate associations for the digits
2 .... shoe
4 .... door
6 .... sticks
8 .... gate

Let's see if we can dream up similar rhyming

associations for the other digits, starting with the hardest, which is 0 (naught or zero). You might try caught if you call the digit 'naught' but I think you'll find a much better choice would be hero to rhyme with 'zero.'

One (1) is easy — make that bun. Two you already have as shoe. Three could be tree. Five rhymes with hive, seven with heaven and nine with wine.

Let's look at the whole list now:

0 = hero
1 = bun
2 = shoe
3 = tree
4 = door
5 = hive
6 = sticks

7 = heaven
8 = gate
9 = wine

By now I won't have to tell you that it isn't the word you should associate, but the picture it conjures up. Use the link method you have already learned to make this easy. Visualise the digit zero being lifted by a brawny hero — a knight in shining armour, a barbarian warrior or whatever type of hero most appeals to you. Now visualise the digit one with a large mouth chomping on a bun. And the digit two with feet pulling on a shoe.

As you go through, make the pictures as clear and appealing as you can. See a tall, bushy tree, a stout wooden door, a busy bee-hive, a pile of sticks you might have gathered for firewood, a chubby little angel playing a harp on a fluffy cloud to represent heaven , a red-painted, wrought-iron garden gate, and a bottle of the very finest vintage wine.

Work on this until just thinking about the digit brings

up the relevant pictorial association.

The other way of doing it, which I personally don't like as well, leap-frogs the rhyme and goes direct to visual associations with the digits themselves. In other words, you take a long hard look at the shape of the digit and see what it reminds you of.

Here again, it is what the shape makes you think of that's important, so do please take the time to work out your own associations. I'll list mine here, just as an example of what I mean. You're welcome to use them if they work for you, but your own would probably be better.

0 = an orange
1 = a thermometer
2 = a duck
3 = the moon
4 = a little girl

5 = a rabbit

6 = a tuba

7 = a war axe

8 = an hour glass

9 = a stylized man

Okay, now you know about creating associations with the basic digits. Let's take a look at how those associations can be put to use. First, you take the number you want to memorise:

7645872955473781463259814

In its present form it is pretty unmemorable. But now you can translate it into visual images, by substituting the pegs you have learned for the digits themselves. In this example, I'll use the rhyming pegs I prefer, but you, of course, should always use the pegs you have learned and favour.

Thus the number...

7645872955473781463259814

... now becomes:

Heaven... sticks... door... hive... gate... heaven... shoe...
wine... hive... hive... door... heaven... tree... heaven...
gate... bun... door... sticks... tree... shoe... hive... wine...
gate... bun... door...

Which may not look all that much better, but bear with
me. Now that you have visual associations, you can at
least make some sort of stab at linking the digits
together in a daisy-chain, or placing them in twenty-
five different locations in your home locus.

The problem, as you'll quickly find, is the repetition of
the same pictures, which does tend to confuse your
memory a little. All the same, you might like to have a
try at remembering that huge number by means of
daisy-chain or locus. Run a quick test on yourself right
now, turn the book over and write down as much of the
number as the system helped you to remember.

When you have completed the test — at least as best

you can — check with the original number and see how well you did, giving yourself one mark for each digit you remembered successfully, in proper sequence, from the left of the number. If you got the whole number correct, scoring 25, then congratulate yourself. You obviously have the sort of brain that takes to training like a duck to water.

How To Set
The Triggers That
Will Detonate
the Memories You Need

Let's get one thing out of the way. You can't clutter up your memory.

This is something that genuinely concerns people. You show them how to memorise shopping lists and they lie awake at night worrying about how they might confuse last week's list with this week's, or get their locus so crowded with junk there just wasn't any more room in there.

But it doesn't happen. Your locus is eternally reusable. You can empty it out a million times and it's always ready for more.

And your link system is just as beautiful. You can forget a list just as easily as you remembered it, allowing it to fade away when you no longer need it. You can memorise a different shopping list every week for a year and never get two of them confused.

Or you can memorise a whole host of different lists and retain every one. All you need to do is put your mind to it. That lump of folded grey matter inside your skull has more storage capacity than the largest computer ever built, maybe even that the largest computer ever likely to be built.

Broadly speaking, you should use locus or link systems to store anything you want to recall in a set sequence. Use the peg system for anything to do with numbers, or anything you want to remember out of sequence.

In many situations, however, just memorising something is not enough — you need to be sure you remember to remember.

You come up against situations like that every day. I meet you in the disco and ask you to tell Sam I need four paper-clips, a floppy disc, half a dozen free range eggs, an Aborigine nose flute, a pair of pink socks, a ball-point pen and a brass Buddha from him urgently.

Thanks to your systems, you memorise the list easily, but you won't actually see Sam until the day after tomorrow. How do you make sure you will remember I asked you to tell him anything? How can you guarantee that you won't be so interested in talking about soccer to Sam that you forget all about what happened at the disco?

The answer is engagingly simple. You form the daisy-chain as usual, then link the first item of your list — in this case the paper-clips — to Sam himself. In your mind's eye, you create a ridiculous association, mentally seeing Sam with paper-clips coming out of his ears. Then you forget the whole thing. This process is called setting a trigger.

The day after tomorrow, when you run into Sam, the trigger you set will detonate automatically and the mere sight of Sam will remind you of paper clips, my conversation with you and, via the daisy chain, with the whole sorry mess of stuff I asked you to tell him I wanted.

On things like shopping trips, you can set a whole series of triggers. On a given day, you may be sallying forth to purchase six textbooks from the bookshop, a dozen items from the supermarket, some DIY stuff from the ironmonger's, a range of modelling equipment from the hobbies shop and four different take-aways from the Chinese restaurant. You also have to remember to call in at the Travel Agent's to pick up your old man's ticket to Bermuda.

You might, of course, daisy chain or peg the whole lot in one long list and work through it in sequence. But that leaves you with a very regimented day with no freedom to mooch about a bit the way you like to. A more freewheeling way to do it would be to create a daisy chain for each place you plan to visit and set a trigger to detonate when you step through the door. That way, you remember what you want as you actually step into the relevant emporium.

The ticket to Bermuda is a bit different, however. The problem isn't remembering what you want when you visit the Travel Agent, since you only want one thing. The problem is remembering to call with the Travel Agent in the first place.

But that problem is no problem. You simply ask yourself which place you definitely will not forget to visit (probably the hobbies shop) and set a trigger reminding you to visit the Travel Agent as you leave. Or the same trigger can be set using a landmark you know you will pass, or a person you know you will meet.

Triggers can be set using anything. One good one is the chime of a church clock. That way you are reminded to do something at a specific time.

In every case, the mechanics are exactly the same. You decide where you want to place your trigger, visualise it clearly, then make a ridiculous link between it and whatever it is you want to remember.

So far, I've kept away from examination situations in the examples and suggestions I've been giving. There's a reason for this. You're likely to face a major examination no more than once in a year, maybe even less. If you count in things like formal class tests, you're probably talking about four times a year at most. This is not a lot of practice situations for the art of memory. More to the point, you want to go into an exam fully practised in the memory arts, not fumbling around building up your experience.

So what you need to do is test, practise and perfect your systems in day to day situations, preferably unimportant situations. Then, when you are skilled, you can move on to more serious work with confidence.

But when you do move on, you will still be using exactly the same techniques, the same systems, applied to rather more important situations. A trigger that works in the supermarket will work just as well in the examination room.

A Dozen
Study Secrets
Guaranteed to Boost
Your School Performance

It's not all memory, of course. To power your way through your exams, you need to know how to study. That's something else they never bother teaching, even though there are certain study secrets that make an enormous difference to the amount of effort you have to put in and the results you achieve.

Fortunately you're going to learn those secrets now. Although they're not, strictly speaking, mindpower techniques, they'll ensure you make most efficient use of your new super memory.

The first secret is going to knock you out.

Study Secret No 1

Make sure you make mistakes.

Isn't that mind-blowing? Isn't that the very last thing

you would think of? But it makes a lot of sense when you hear the reasoning behind it. The reasoning behind it is this:

You live in a world where everybody's big into achievement. The great goal is something called success. That's what your folks want you to have. That's what your friends want you to have. That's probably what you want you to have.

Which is fine, except the yearning for success has stopped people thinking straight about failure. Almost everybody I know thinks failure has something to do with making mistakes.

But failure isn't about making mistakes. It's about falling short of a particular goal, a process which may sometimes involve mistakes, but can equally well come about through lack of energy, illness, a change in your priorities, a decision that you no longer want to achieve what you once wanted to achieve, or a dozen and one other factors.

Mistakes, on the other hand, are part of being human. They are inevitable ... and extremely useful. They are, in fact, probably the most useful learning tool there is.

The first Study Secret forces you to face the fact you will make mistakes, even encourages you to welcome them so you can learn from them. But most of all, it advises you to rest easy with your mistakes.

This doesn't mean you should ignore them. Correct them, learn from them, then forget them. The more often you do that during study, the less often you'll have to do it during an exam. And you'll be a lot more relaxed about your performance, which has to be a benefit as well.

Study Secret No 2

Don't butterfly.

I know you have a lot of ground to cover, a lot of things to do, but research shows that if you move from one study project to another in bite-size pieces, your retention goes to bits.

So in order to achieve maximum recall from your super memory techniques, plan to work your way completely through one project before starting on another.

Study Secret No 3

Cut out external stimulus.

This is hardly a secret at all. Everybody knows you study best in a quiet room without interruptions.

Study Secret No 4

Keep a snack handy.

I thought you'd like that. But it's sensible advice. There is a definite relationship between what you eat and how well you remember.

The real bugbear when it comes to study is blood sugar.

Put simply, if your levels of blood sugar drop too low, your concentration nosedives and your memory blows a fuse.

Blood sugar is exactly what it sounds like — the amount of sugar present in your blood at any given time. Blood sugar rises after a meal, drops when you get hungry. The feeling of hunger is actually your body's signal that blood sugar is getting low. That's why sucking a sweet will usually banish hunger as quickly as a full meal.

You can trigger a fast, dramatic rise in blood sugar by eating cake, sweets, chocolates, most breakfast cereals (which tend to have sugar added in their manufacture) drinking a whole variety of soft drinks, or by taking sugar direct — in tea, for example.

Unfortunately, blood sugar raised in this way does not stay high very long.

So while keeping a snack handy as you study (to ensure adequate blood sugar levels) is obviously a good idea, the type of snack is important. Anything which contains refined sugar will give you a quick lift, but won't hold your levels long. Fruit is better.

But best of all is a protein snack. You get protein in things like peanuts, soya products, lentils, meat, poultry and fish. A protein snack raises blood sugar levels more slowly than cake or fruit, but keeps them higher for far longer.

In other words, a protein snack helps you maintain your optimum memory performance throughout the whole of your study period. It's a good idea to copy the condemned man and eat a hearty (protein) breakfast on the day of your exam as well. You may not feel like it, but it will keep your blood sugar regulated.

Study Secret No 5

Don't smoke.

Apart from causing cancer and heart attacks in later life, smoking is screwing up your memory right now.

Research in the States has shown conclusively that people who don't smoke have a 24% better level of recall than those who do. British research strongly suggests that smoking adversely effects the length of time you can remember things as well.

Study Secret No 6

Take a little exercise before you study or enter an exam.

Lack of physical exercise doesn't seem to affect how well you remember something , but it does slow down the time it takes for you to recall it.

But don't be tempted to take too much exercise before your study period or your exam. You'll see why in the next secret.

Study Secret No 7

Don't study when you're over- tired.

And obviously try to avoid taking exams in that condition too.

Study Secret No. 8

Relax.

Tension blocks memory. If you've ever had a name or a fact on the tip of your tongue, you know the last thing you can do is force it. Relax and think of something else and chances are you'll remember. Get tense and you'll never remember.

Of course, everybody tells you to relax, but nobody tells you how. Until now.

Starting tomorrow morning and continuing each morning thereafter, I would suggest you to set aside a short period for the practice of relaxation.

How much time you spend is up to you, but anything less than 10 minutes isn't really worthwhile; and anything above half an hour is a bit over the top.

Conduct your relaxation session in an upright chair. Don't lie down on a couch or bed: you'll only fall asleep.

Begin by regulating your breathing. Relaxation is a physical function. Your muscles use oxygen extracted from your bloodstream. Your bloodstream, in turn, extracts that oxygen from the air you breathe. By regulating your breathing, you increase the oxygen available in your blood, your muscles extract the optimum amount and are far happier to relax for you.

Here's how to do it:

1. Breathe in to the mental count of four...

2. Hold your breath in to the mental count of two...

3. Breathe out to the mental count of four...

4. Hold your breath out to the mental count of two.

Get your breathing comfortable before you go on to the second part of the exercise.

Once you have established a comfortable rhythm of 2/4 Breathing, let it run for about three minutes, then start the following relaxation sequence. (If you can hold the 2/4 rhythm while you do it, that's great, but chances are you will not be able to do so at first.If so, just start your session with three minutes of 2/4 breathing, then go back to normal breathing while you carry out the main relaxation sequence, then take up 2/4 breathing again when you are nicely relaxed.)

Concentrate on your feet. Wiggle them about. Curl them to tense the muscles, then allow them to relax.

Concentrate next on your calf muscles. Tighten and relax them.

Concentrate on your thigh muscles. Tighten and relax them.

Concentrate on your buttock muscles. Tighten your buttocks and anus, then relax them.

Do the same with your stomach, hands, arms, back, chest and shoulders.

Concentrate on your neck. Tighten the muscles then relax them.

Concentrate on your face. Grit your teeth and contort your features to tense up the facial muscles then relax them.

Concentrate on your scalp. From to tighten the scalp muscles, then relax them.

Now tighten up every muscle in your body, holding your entire body momentarily rigid, then relax, letting go as completely as you are able. Do this final whole body sequence again, then again — three times in all. On the third time, take a really deep breath when you tense the muscles and sigh deeply aloud as you let the tension go.

Use the technique regularly until you have trained yourself to relax totally any time you want to ... including the exam room.

Study Secret No 9

Cram.

If your only interest is to pass a particular exam, the

evidence suggests cramming will help.

But one word of warning. Cramming is a short-term technique. It gets information into your head for a particular exam at a cost — and the cost is that a month after the exam, you will have forgotten most of it. Your memory techniques may help in this, but don't bet on it.

So if you decide to cram, be fully aware you are engaged on an exercise solely designed to help you get through an examination — you aren't really learning anything.

Study Secret No 10

Ask yourself questions.

This is a very simple, but remarkably little-known technique. If you want to absorb material from a book, most people will advise you to read and reread it time and time again.

It's bad advice. What you should do is read the material, then ask yourself questions about the content.

This does three things.

First, it actively helps you remember the material.

Next, it pin-points those areas where your understanding or recall is weak, enabling you to revise far more efficiently.

Finally, it acts as a powerful reassurance. If you are able to recall the material well enough to answer your own questions, you have increased your chances of recalling that material in an examination.

Study Secret No 11

Keep your periods of study consistent.

I don't know why this is, but if you alternate between long and short periods of study, you will remember less than if you divide your study time up into (at least roughly) equal periods.

Study Secret No 12

Your most efficient study period is one hour per day.

I don't suppose they'll thank me for telling you that one, but it happens to be true.

Back in 1978 there was a study carried out on, of all people, British postmen. This showed conclusively that those who studied one hour per day learned twice as fast as those who studied four hours a day, broken into two two-hour sessions.

The important message here is efficiency. And continuity.

The Five
Hidden Structures
That Can Help You
Remember What You Read

Many — maybe even most — examinations are tests of what you have read about something. So what's the best way to remember what you read?

Before you even start to use your mindpower memory techniques, the way you approach what you read can make a huge difference to what you remember — and even how much of it you understand.

Like so much we've already examined, this goes back to the way your mind works. It's obvious that if you know something well, you will remember it better. But what isn't often realised is that if you know the structure of something, if, that is, you know it's basic shape, this helps you remember even if you don't actually know the thing itself.

We may seem a long way from your reading material, but we're not. When you're writing a factual book, there are only so many ways you can organise the information. Of these, experts have unearthed five basic patterns that come up time and time again.

The Step Pattern

This is the simplest of all five basic patterns and by far the easiest to recognise. Sometimes it is actually labelled for you. How often have you come across a series of instructions in a book that go:

Step 1: Take a piece of square paper and fold it across both diagonals.

Step 2: Fold the corners in towards the middle.

Step 3: Turn the folded paper over and crease horizontally.

Step 4: Crumple up the whole mess and throw it in the fire.

Even where the pattern is not set out like this, it is always easy to recognise. You simply keep a weather eye out for information organised in stages one stage building on the other.

The Aspect Pattern

Like the Step Pattern, the Aspect Pattern is open-ended — that is to say it can run to any length. It approaches a given subject by breaking it down into its component aspects and presenting these one after another.

Perhaps the most fruitful place to look for the Aspect Pattern is in any encyclopaedia, since it is very widely used in these works. This example of the Aspect Pattern is taken from the Encyclopaedia Britannica:

Virgil

Virgil was regarded by the Romans as their greatest poet, an estimation that subsequent generations have upheld ....

Political background

During Virgil's youth, as the Roman Republic neared its end, the political and military situation in Italy was confused and often calamitous ....

Literary career

Some of Virgil's earliest poetry may have survived in a

collection of poems attributed to him and known as the *Appendix Vergiliana* ....

Influence and reputation

Virgil's poetry immediately became famous in Rome and was admired by the Romans for two main reasons ....

Major works

Eclogae (42-37 BC; *Eclogues*) comprising ten poems also known as the *Bucolica. Georgica* (36 - 29 BC; *Georgics*) comprising four books ....

You have only to look at that example for the Aspect Pattern to become clear. The article moves from a brief overall introduction to Aspect 1, which was Virgil's political background, then to Aspect 2, his literary career; and so on.

It is very easy to see the Aspect Pattern in works like Britannica, which tend to itemise the aspects in subheadings, as happened in this example. Other works may not be so helpful, but even without subheadings, the Aspect Pattern remains easy to spot.

An article on the Welsh landscape, for example, takes us through the aspects of its geographical relief (Aspect 1), soils and drainage (Aspect 2), climate (Aspect 3) and finally vegetation (Aspect 4.)

The Problem Analysis Pattern

This is a four-stage pattern commonly used in discussion documents.

The Problem Analysis Pattern is as follows:

PROBLEM
|
EFFECTS
|
CAUSES
|
SOLUTIONS

As a quick example, you might feel inspired to write an essay on your current situation, structured around the Problem Analysis Pattern. If you did, it would run along the lines:

Problem: I have a rotten memory.

Effects: I am likely to fail my exams.

Causes: My mother dropped me on my head as
             a baby.

Solution: I am studying mindpower.

The Scientific Pattern

This is a three-stage Thesis/Proof/Conclusion pattern
often found in scientific works — hence its name.

It begins with the statement of a particular idea (the
thesis) which may or may not be true, but is deemed
worthy of consideration. An example might be the
notion, now widely published on cigarette packets, that
smoking seriously damages your health.

Having established the idea under consideration, the
pattern then proceeds to look for evidence which tends
to confirm or refute the thesis (the proof). In our
smoking example, this might be a review of research
into the clear statistical linkage between cigarette
smoking and lung cancer, or evidence that smokers
have a greater likelihood to develop heart disease.

With the case presented and established (or refuted) the Pattern then draws a reasonable conclusion from everything that has gone before — e.g. you should give up fags or learn to breathe without your lungs.

The Propaganda Pattern

In many ways, this pattern is similar to the Scientific Pattern, with which it is often confused. But the key to telling them apart is the fact that while the Scientific Pattern puts forward a thesis, which may or may not be true, and sets out to determine which, the Propaganda Pattern puts forward an opinion and seeks to persuade you that it is valid.

Like the Scientific, this too is a three-stage pattern:

OPINION
|
PERSUASION
|
RECOMMENDATION

As an example, the pattern might begin with the opinion that Donald Duck should be Britain's next Prime Minister.

Eccentric though the opinion might be, it can nonetheless be backed by the persuasive arguments that ducks don't start wars or support cuts in the Health Service.

The recommendation is obvious — vote for Donald Duck at the next election.

A knowledge of these five common patterns will help you discover the hidden structures of the material you read and thus remember its content more easily. But knowing the patterns is not enough — you have to look for them (and find them.)

It is only when you take the trouble to find the patterns that the material you are reading takes on the familiar shape that is easier for you to remember.

But suppose you come across material that is not organised in any of the five patterns — is not organised in any pattern you can discover?

It happens. The world is full of badly written books. If you are forced to learn from some of them, your best bet is to extract the information they give and restructure it in the most suitable of the five patterns.

Do this in your head, if you can, or by rewriting the material if you can't.

It may sound like hard work, but the bottom line is still that you will remember better.

Why You Can Afford to Ignore 80% of Everything You Read and Still Absorb Enough to Pass Your Next Exam

Most students approach articles and textbooks with the firm conviction that they should, ideally, try to remember everything they read in them.

But this is a pretty dumb idea when you think it through.

The whole art of communicating information is to take the new stuff and relate it to what the reader already knows and understands. That way you have a fighting chance that the new material will become known and understood as well.

There is no such thing as an article or textbook containing 100% new material. You wouldn't understand it if there was.

You can check this out for yourself very easily. Just wander down to your local reference library and take out the most advanced book you can find on something about which you know absolutely nothing. (My personal favourite is the mathematical arguments against Einstein's initial presentation of his Unified Field Theory.)

Even if you manage to read the book, you will quickly find you still know absolutely nothing by the time you've finished. The writer has failed to communicate with you, however much (s)he knew about the subject.

And the reason for this failure of communication was that, as an advanced textbook, the work made no attempt to relate new information to what you already knew, because the writer assumed you knew far more than you actually did.

Buckminster Fuller, who made a study of these things, suggested that the ideal balance in a book was 20% new ideas related to 80% familiar material. He had found the majority of readers favoured this mix and books that achieved it tended to become popular.

Not all books and articles achieve this ideal, of course, but if they are going to be understood at all, they have to have some balance between the old and the new.

And this fact can cut right down on the amount of work you have to do when reading.

Try approaching your next study period with the mindset of a miner prospecting for gold. You know there's some about somewhere, but you still have to dig it out of the mountain.

You can encourage this mindset by deciding in advance what it is that you want to extract from it, then move in to search out the (relatively) small percentage of new information that is relevant to your theme.

By approaching the project this way, you can elect to absorb only enough comparisons and analogies to allow you to understand the new material. And you can avoid wasting time on diversions which, however interesting, do not fall into the category of information you have decided to extract.

Once again, this approach has very little to do with education which, if it means anything at all, surely means expanding your mind into as many different areas as possible.

But it has a lot to do with efficiency in the way you

study; and consequently has a lot to do with how much effort you must invest in order to pass your next examination.

The Key Word System
of Extracting Facts to
Burn into Your Memory

Even your new super memory, finely honed to deal with lists and numbers and what have you, can't be much help if you're trying to remember, say, a literary critique of The Tempest of a detailed exposition of the composition of quasars.

Or can it?

In fact, if you marry your mindpower memory systems to the Fact-Extraction Method I'm about to outline, you can go a long way towards remembering just about anything you want.

The marriage is particularly useful in a revision situation, where you are familiar with the basic material, but are desperate to ensure it sticks in your mind long enough to get you through next week's exam.

It can also be used, with stunning effect, in any

preparations you may have to make for oral examinations. (Or, come to that, preparations for debates and public speeches.)

This approach needs a little more work than several of the techniques you've been using lately, but the results are well worth it.

Let's assume for the sake of this example that you're moving inexorably towards a geography exam. You've checked through past papers and have come to the chilling conclusion that the most likely questions to be asked in the exam will be about somewhere really obscure, like the People's Republic of Yemen.

You open your textbook and find a long chapter on the Yemen which you have never quite gotten around to reading before. It goes on for page after tightly printed page, like the small type in a legal contract.

So how do you go about remembering the information?

You start by reading right through the chapter once. No memory tricks, no visualisation, no big effort to try to make it stick. All you're doing is familiarising yourself with the overall picture.

When you've read it through once, read it through again, this time looking for the basic pattern of the information. (See The Five Hidden Structures That Can Help You Remember What You Read.) Chances are you'll find it's organised in the Aspect Pattern, but if not, analyse it thoroughly until you find the actual pattern for yourself.

Once you have the pattern, start digging for Key Words.

A Key Word is a single word that stands for a whole block of information. For example, the main geographical feature of Yemen is its long coastal belt, running a full 740 miles along the northern shore of the Gulf of Aden from the southern entrance to the Red Sea in the west to the Oman frontier in the east. The Key Word for this information is coast.

When you start to study up on the national economy, you find it is mainly dependent on the single port of Aden, which acts as a sort of 'service station' to the region. Outside of Aden, the economy is almost exclusively agricultural. Key Words here are obviously Aden and farm.

Work your way through the information like this,

selecting the Key Words for each aspect in turn.

When you have selected your Key Words, turn each into a visualisation. If you have any which do not lend themselves to easy visualisation — like Aden — use word-swap. Thus Aden might remind you of Eden (the Garden of) allowing a visualisation of Adam and Eve. Or you might split it into a den in which case you would visualise the lair of a wild animal.

If you are satisfied that the Key Word is enough to call up its associated information, then all you have to do now is daisy-chain the Key Words. That way, by dragging up your daisy chain during the examination you can move step by logical step through the textbook article you have read.

If, however, you find that the Key Word does not immediately call up everything you have read on the subject, daisy-chain the relevant information with the Key Word instead.

For example, you might daisy chain cattle, sheep, goats, camels and donkeys to the Key Word farm since these are the main animals involved in the rural economy. You might remind yourself that a substantial number of sheep and goats are imported by visualising them walking over the sea.

Aden's service station economy could be recalled by a daisy-chain visualisation of a modern service station in the Garden of Eden, with Eve pumping apples into the tank of Adam's Volkswagen.

If you decide to daisy-chain information to the Key Words, use your locus to link the Key Words themselves. You can do a two-way daisy-chain, linking a Key Word with a string of information in one direction and with the next Key Word in another. But there is always the possibility of confusion, so why run risks?

The Key Word system can be used successfully on almost any type of textbook article. When you become really familiar with it, you'll find you can actually select Key Words and make the relevant chains as you go along. I know that may sound pretty far-fetched to you now, but the whole point about Mindpower is that it retrains you in the way you think.

There is nothing unnatural about this, any more than there is anything particularly natural about the way you think at the moment. The way you think at the moment is mainly a matter of upbringing, early training and habit. As the new ways become habitual they will become more and more easy until eventually they get to be second nature to you.

Once that happens, you won't even have to think about applying Mindpower techniques, you'll do so instinctively — and very, very quickly.

The interesting thing about the Key Word system is that you can apply it not only to material you want to absorb and remember, but to material you create yourself.

How often have you prepared a project in advance of an exam, only to find you couldn't remember a word of it when the big day came?
How often have you written a paper for an oral exam, a speech for your debating society, then stood up to deliver with your mouth gasping like a fish and your mind a total blank?

The Key Word System puts a stop to that sort of nonsense once and for all. You can use it exactly the way you used it in the example given above. That is, you can write down your speech or your project, then analyse it for its basic information pattern and dig out the relevant Key Words.

Chances are since it's your own work, you will only need to daisy-chain the Key Words to one another. But if you are feeling particularly nervous, you can go the whole hog, daisy-chain each Key Word to its associated information, then place each Key Word in your current working locus.

Alternatively, you can save yourself trouble by consciously building your speech or project around Key Words. This can be a great way of getting something down on paper (since it forces you to organise your thoughts in advance) and it certainly saves you the trouble of extracting Key Words afterwards.

Suppose, for example, you were preparing a piece on the Duke of Wellington. Your Key Words might include

*Dublin ... where he was born

*India ... where he developed as a soldier

*Salamanca ... where he trounced 40,000 French troops at the rate of 1,000 a minute

*Napoleon ... his greatest enemy

*Waterloo ... where he beat Napoleon

*Liverpool... to remind you he joined the Earl of

Liverpool's Tory Cabinet
*Prime Minister ... which was the post he achieved in 1828.

Having selected your Key Words, you would then daisy-chain them with aspects of associated information — the Irish influence on the Duke's early life, the change in him when he served in India and Napoleon's mistake in dismissing him as a 'Sepoy General', how he became involved in the European wars, and so on.

Remember that you have brain cells as numerous as the stars in the sky and the sands of the desert, so you are not going to overburden your memory no matter how many facts you stuff in there.

When you have your project finished and the daisy chains established, stuff the whole lot into a visualisation of a Wellington boot. It may be an undignified way to think of one of Britain's greatest soldiers, but it will certainly help you remember all about him.

How to Build A Mind
That Positively
Explodes with Information

Just about everything you're expected to learn bristles with facts.

Who ran naked down the street in Greece shouting 'Eureka!' — and what was he making all the fuss about?

Who discovered the properties of radium?

Where was the site of the world's greatest ever explosion?

What does the square on the hypotenuse equal?

And so on, ad (almost) infinitum.

But it's not enough to know the answers. It's often necessary to relate the facts to other things as well.

That old boy running naked down the street, for

instance, is a part of Greek history (a disputed part, but a part nonetheless) but his real importance is to physics.

(I can hardly believe anyone doesn't know the story, but just in case: the Greek Archimedes is reputed to have become so excited by discovering that immersing himself in his bath displaced an equal volume of water that he ran naked down the street shouting 'I've found it!' When they released him from the funny farm he formulated the Principle of Archimedes still taught to this day.)

Madame Curie's work on radium has implications for medicine (it killed her), physics (she had discovered radioactivity), politics (who's got the biggest bomb?), military strategy (who's got the biggest bomb?) and history.

The site of the world's greatest explosion — Siberia — is related to forestry, ecology and agriculture on the one hand (because it destroyed so much wood and farmland) and astronomy on the other (because it seems to have been caused by a collision between the Earth and a meteor.)

At school, the facts you have to learn are often related

to people. Who unified Germany? Where did General Gordon get his comeuppance? What theory did Einstein put forward? That sort of thing.

And where they're not related to people, they're generally related to each other. Question: what were the implications of the development of transistor technology? Answer: we all started to carry little cheap radios about.

With the work you've done so far, remembering linkages has to be a piece of cake. All you do is make a ludicrous association between them and visualise it in your mind.

If the things being linked aren't easily pictured, then you convert them into something close that is, or peg them onto something else that is.

Let's see how these basic principles can be put to work to cram your head full of facts on just about any subject you might be taught. We'll start with facts related to people and take, as our example, one of the most energetic Germans of them all, good old Otto von Bismarck.

There are a lot of things you might want to link with

Bismarck — the fact that he was sent as ambassador to Leningrad, the fact that he became Prime Minister in Berlin, the Franco-German War of 1870-71 — but to keep it simple, we'll confine the historical bit to the one big important thing: the fact that he unified Germany.

Your first job is to picture Bismarck.

There are a number of ways you can go about this. You might, for example, actually know what he looked like. I read in a novel somewhere that he was a big ugly brute with close-cropped hair and duelling scars on his face, but that may not be true. Or you might have seen a movie sometime in which he was played by Eddie Murphy or John Cleese.

In other words, you might be able immediately to put a face to the name. If so, you can start visualising right away.

But the chances are you won't be able to put a face to the name. I studied history for years and I still don't know what Count Cavour looked like, what Robert the Bruce looked like, what Philip of Spain looked like; and I only think I know what Henry VIII, Napoleon and Atilla the Hun looked like from television programmes about them.

If you can't put a face to the name (or can't be absolutely certain you will always remember the name by visualising the face) then you have to make a specialised use of the Word-Swap System.

You do this by taking the (meaningless and impossible to visualise) name Bismarck and converting it into something that can be visualised. If you have an old-fashioned mind like mine, you might break it down into besom (a sort of broom made from twigs) and ark (the ship that Noah sailed in.) Or you might mentally animate a pencil mark on a piece of paper so that it scurries busily here and there — a busy mark.

Perhaps the best visualisation of all, if you happen to be familiar with the basic unit of German currency, would be to visualise a one-mark coin scurrying around busily — another version of busy mark which carries the German association in itself.

Your next step is to visualise the unification of Germany. That one's easy. All you need do is see a fragmented map of Germany in your mind's eye, then have that busy little mark zipping about pushing all the pieces together.

The great thing about fact-links is that they work both ways.

What was Bismarck's major claim to fame? Bismarck becomes the busy mark which you immediately visualise as pushing Germany together. So Bismarck's major claim to fame was the unification of Germany.

Who unified Germany? Your mind pictures Germany in a fragmented state and at once into the mental picture races that busy mark to put it all together again. Busy Mark — I beg your pardon: Bismarck — was the one who unified Germany.

You can use this system to link any sort of fact to any person, living or dead.

What country did Hitler invade in 1939 to start World War Two? You can picture Uncle Adolf doing a ridiculous goose-step up and down a pole to remind you it was the invasion of Poland that started the hassle.

Who finally defeated Napoleon? Visualise the little Corsican squashed by a Wellington boot.

Who were the first men to climb Everest? They were, of course, that uptight opera singer Tensing (tense sing) and his sick, hirsute companion Hilary (ill hairy) who paused frequently to — are you ready for this? — have a rest! (Everest.)

A lot of your visualisations will turn into bad puns like that, but what matter if they help you remember?

You do not, of course, have to confine yourself to single linkages. You can daisy-chain a whole host of associated facts together. Maybe it's important to remember Hilary's nationality. If so, daisy chain a kiwi to remind you he's from New Zealand. Who was the leader of the expedition? Add a link showing a fox-hunt galloping all over the mountain to remind you it was Sir John Hunt.

Is there a chance of getting confused as you link more and more facts together? Go back to our very first example, for instance. Bismarck is not just the Iron Chancellor — it's the capital of North Dakota, a German battleship in World War II, a range of mountains in New Guinea, a sea that forms part of the Pacific Ocean and an archipelago in that sea.

Given all the things that Bismarck might be, isn't there a grave danger your linkages are going to end up like a ball of wool after the cat's got at it?

In fact, as you'll quickly discover, this simply doesn't happen. The question of context comes in here. Link words and daisy chains aside, if somebody asks you who unified Germany, you don't start wondering if it was that battleship in World War II. (Unless you're very thick.)

Exactly the same mechanism comes into play when you have constructed your daisy chains. You can even, if you wish, chain the battleship Bismarck with the man Bismarck and the sea Bismarck without the least worry about getting them confused.

I'll go further. You can chain the battleship Bismarck and all its daisy-chained associations with the man Bismarck and all his associations and any other Bismarck you feel like throwing in there .... and you still won't mix them up.

What you have inside your head is the most marvellous filing cabinet on earth. It has storage capacity that is truly staggering and retrieval systems so efficient they would take your breath away.

Even without any special training, t
hese systems enable you routinely to differentiate between things that should, on the face of it, prove very confusing.

That's why the context enables you to read the word invalid and decide at once whether it means something that is not valid or somebody who is ill.

That's why you can half hear the sound sore and decide whether it means painful, what a bird does when it flies, or something you use to cut through wood.

Context does not go away when you start to pack your mind with facts. Nor do your routine mental systems. If you don't find something confusing before you train your mind, you certainly won't find it confusing afterwards.

With that reassurance, we can no move on from linking people with their accomplishments to linking facts with facts.

Assume for a moment that you desperately need to

remember the habitat of the button quail — which is, in fact, scrubby grasslands in the warmer regions of Europe.

Your first step, exactly as before, is to visualise the button quail itself. It may be, of course, that your ornithological studies have already given you a very clear picture of what this little six inch long dull-coloured bird looks like. You might consequently be able to visualise it making its typical crouched, zigzagging run through the grass or breaking into a weak, whirring flight on short, rounded wings.

But there are fifteen species of these birds, each of which looks at least a little different from the other, so straightforward visualisation of the actual bird may not prove all that easy or effective. Perhaps it would be better to create your mental picture direct from the bird's name.

In this instance, that is a particularly easy exercise — you don't even need to bring in word-swap. All you have to do is visualise a trembling button — a button that quails in the face of danger.

Now you move on to visualising the habitat — not as it

110

is, but rather in a form that can help you form a ridiculous association. The habitat is scrubby grassland in warmer regions — an environment nicely encapsulated in the words warm scrub.

And those two words call up their own picture — indeed, their own linkage. All you need to do is visualise a trembling button sweating profusely while it scrubs a rock under a blazing sun. The link is there and from now on you need never forget that the button quail is associated with scrubland in the warmer regions.

One more:

You have to remember that the chromosphere is the lowest layer of the sun's atmosphere.

The word chromosphere isn't one that crops up every day in conversation and at first sight you might imagine it would be a difficult one to visualise. Not a bit of it. You know perfectly well a sphere is a round ball and chrome is the shiny metal they put on cars to make them sell better.

So visualising a chrome sphere should drive the unusual new term into your head very effectively. How do you link it to the sun? Simple, you visualise yourself sunbathing under a chrome sphere up there in the sky.

Now you've linked chromosphere with the sun, but how do you complete the linkage so you know it's the bottom layer of the sun's atmosphere? Well, a layer is a hen, so you could visualise two hens standing on top of the chrome sphere — and on top of one another. The bottom one should be flapping her wings to draw attention to herself.

The whole picture is perfectly ludicrous ... and for that very reason, it works. The low hen is the bottom layer. The chrome sphere is up there in place of the sun. And another fact is tattooed indelibly onto your brain.

The Complete
Memory System and
How You Can Start to Use It

If you've worked this far through the book, you have as much basic memory training as you're ever going to need in order to skate through most of your exams.

You can go further if you like. In his book How to Develop a Super-Power Memory, Harry Lorayne suggests you should use the phonetic figure system to develop at least 100 visual pegs which you should commit to memory in advance of using them. And if you want to do this, there's no reason why you shouldn't.

But even if you don't, what you have learned so far is more than enough to put you in total control of your memory banks for most practical purposes. Let's review where you're at now, step by step.

1. There are two parts to memory — filing away the information in the first place and recalling it again later.

You could draw the parts like this:

MEMORY

Starts Here   Ends Here

Filing Away   Recalling

2. Any effort you put into the right hand side of that diagram is largely wasted. The place to put the effort is the left. In other words, if you want to remember, the time to put in the effort is when you are filing away information, not when you are trying to recall it. This is the exact opposite of the way most people try to remember.

3. Memorising the old way, by repeating something over and over, if difficult and inefficient. The sooner you break the habit of trying to memorise that way, the faster you will start to build a better memory.

4. Visualisation is the real key to memory. If you can file something visually, you make it much, much easier to remember.

5. If you exaggerate, dramatise or make your visualisation ridiculous, it becomes easier still to remember.

6. Anything that has meaning is far easier to remember that something that hasn't.

7. Attention, interest and observation all contribute to effective memory.

8. If you can't remember something, peg it to something else that you can.

9. If you have to remember something meaningless, like a long number, convert it into something — or a number of things — meaningful.

By now, you should have converted those bits and pieces into three fundamental memory systems, all involving visualisation —

The Locus System involves creating a place in your mind in which you can store items you wish to remember. This place can be a visualisation of your own home or of some other, larger building, which may or may not be based on physical reality. A variation of the system lets you create a highly portable, short-list locus by mentally placing items you wish to remember on various parts of your own body.

The Link or Daisy-Chain System involves the use of visualisation to create exaggerated and ridiculous links between one item and another, so that recalling one item will automatically drag up the associated links.

The Peg System shows how you can remember something difficult, like a number, by converting it into something easier and more meaningful to visualise. At a basic level, you can convert the ten digits 0 - 9 into pictures either through rhyming associations or through visual associations suggested by the actual shapes of the figures. A far more advanced version of the Peg System associates certain sounds with each digit so that you can create words which you can then visualise to help you remember any number.

In practice, as your super memory starts to develop, you'll find these systems aren't really separate. You can mix and match as much as you like and gradually developing your own custom-built system that is really comfortable for you.

You've already seen something of this earlier — as, for example, when you store the first item of a daisy chain in your locus. But the blending of the systems goes a lot further.

Suppose for some reason you want to remember a list of items in such a way that you can recall instantly the first, or the fifth or the 10th item on that list. To keep the example simple, here's a list of ten straightforward items ... but your list, theoretically, can be any size at all:

Library book
Postage stamp
Pair of pyjamas
Bottle of lemonade
Pair of scissors
Fountain pen
Deck of cards
Comb
Toothbrush
Pot of jam

Remembering the list itself is no problem — you could use either the locus or the link methods for that. But neither method will help you recall a particular item by number. You might, I suppose, count the links in your daisy chain or the rooms in your locus and get the right answer that way, but it would be slow and cumbersome in a lengthy list and a perfect example of putting effort into the right hand side of the diagram when you should really have put it on the left.

To recall numbered items from a list, you have to file away that list in a particular way. Instead of associating the list items with each other, as in the daisy chain, or with a particular place, as in the locus, you have to associate them with their relevant number. So at the time you make the effort to remember, your list becomes:

1. Library book
2. Postage stamp
3. Pair of pyjamas
4. Bottle of lemonade
5. Pair of scissors
6. Fountain pen
7. Deck of cards
8. Comb
9. Toothbrush
10. Pot of jam

This is only the first step, of course, since the numbers in themselves are far too difficult to memorise. Your next step is to convert the numbers into their visual equivalents. As I mentioned earlier, I rather fancy the rhyming associations, so I'll use those for the digits 1 to 9 on this list. Making the conversion, the list becomes:

1. BUN ... Library Book
2. SHOE ... Postage Stamp
3. TREE ... Pair of Pyjamas
4. DOOR ... Bottle of lemonade
5. HIVE ... Pair of scissors
6. STICKS ... Fountain pen
7. HEAVEN ... Deck of cards
8. GATE ... Comb
9. WINE ... Toothbrush

For the final number of the list, I'll go to my phonetic links — the sounds T or D for 1 and S or Z for 0. This leaves me with a large number of word possibilities — teas, doze, dose, daisy etc. The one I'll pick is toes. This follows the logic of the phonetic system, but carries an additional association with the number 10 since that happens to be the number of toes I am equipped with. So ...

(10) TOES ... Pot of jam

Having gotten this far, you use the Link Method to associate your number word with your list item.

Starting with 1 (bun) you might visualise yourself visiting a library where the shelves were full of buns instead of books. Or you might see yourself using a sticky bun as a bookmark. Or absentmindedly eating a library book you have pulled out of a bag of buns.

As you can see, the associations are made in exactly the same way as before — by ridiculous, exaggerated or substituted visualisations.

For 2 (shoe) you might visualise your shoe covered in postage stamps. Or imagine yourself trying to glue a shoe onto a little in place of a stamp.

Go through the rest of the list in this way, creating a ridiculous association link between the item and the number picture in each case. When you have finished, test yourself by having somebody call out a number between one and 10. As they do, your mind will run a fast two-stage link: 'One' becomes 'Bun' and 'Bun' instantly reminds you of a library book. Thus item 1 on the list is 'Library book'.

With a little bit of practice, you'll find you can remember long lists this way; and since the associations are a two-way street, you'll not only be able to name item 7 (or item 70) instantly, but you will also be able to tell people the correct number when they give you an item from the list.

If you've worked your way through this example, your memory training is now complete. The systems you have so far learned are all the tools you will need to build a prodigious memory in the weeks and months ahead.

The rest of this book just shows you how to use the systems in various different situations. Notably the sort of situations that will get you through exams.

How to Astonish
Your Teachers When
They Set Your Next Exam

If you've come this far, you deserve a small reward.
This section is it. It contains a technique which you will
find utterly useless in any examination you may sit and
totally without benefit in your study sessions.

But it will impress the pants off anybody you try it on.

The way it works is this:

You're sitting in class idly recalling the entire Table of
Elements forwards and backwards, then your teacher
announces your next examination will be held on
October 23.

You glance up and murmur quietly, "That's a Monday,
isn't it?"

And when the calendar is checked, you're right! What's
more, you can reel off, almost instantly, the day of any
date throughout the year.

How's it done?

It requires a little preparation. Find a calendar and use it to discover the date of the first Sunday of each month throughout the year.

In 1989, for example, the first Sunday of January was on January 1, the first Sunday of February was February 5, the first Sunday of March was March 5, the first Sunday of April was April 2 and so on.

Write down the numbers of those first Sundays, giving you a twelve digit number for the year. In 1989 that twelve digit number was:

155274263153

Now use the techniques you've learned to memorise that one. When you have it burned in, you're ready.

When the teacher tells you that the next examination is on October 23, you consult your memorised number and find (in 1989) that the first Sunday in October falls on October 1.
Armed with that information, you can calculate that the second Sunday falls on October 8, the third on October

15 and the fourth on October 22. You do this by adding seven for each succeeding week.

(Actually you wouldn't do it week by week once you get the hang of it. Trying to find the day for October 23, you'd add 21 — which is 3x7 — to your initial 1 and find directly that the third Sunday was October 22.)

Since October 22 is a Sunday, it follows that the 23rd, the day following, has to be a Monday.

If anybody ask you how you are able to put days onto dates so easily, lie a little. Tell them you've memorised the entire year's calendar.

After all, you could now if you really wanted to.

Sheep Ahoy!

GRAHAM MARKS AND
CHRISTOPHER MAYNARD

A hilarious collection of extraordinary but absolutely true stories – stranger than fiction – culled from the back pages and people columns of newspapers.

£1.95 ☐

Mispronts

GRAHAM MARKS AND
CHRISTOPHER MAYNARD

An amusing selection of silly misprints from newspapers and magazines.

£1.95 ☐

Odd Pets

GRAHAM MARKS AND
CHRISTOPHER MAYNARD

A useful collection of outlandish pets, specially compiled for the lazy pet owner who is not excited by the idea of cleaning out, grooming and feeding. All of the pets to be found in this book are easily obtained, either from the wild, or the human body, and require the minimum of care and maintenance.

£1.95 ☐

ARMADA

Crazy Curriculum
JONATHAN CLEMENTS

A hilarious alternative look at school education, including study notes on traditional subjects such as history, and not so usual ones such as human behaviour. There are also exam papers and answers, quizzes, timetables and school reports of famous people.

£1.95 ☐

Writing Jokes and Riddles
BILL HOWARD

This is a joke book with a difference – it actually teaches you how to make up a joke! Interspersed with plenty of hilarious examples it also contains a list of key words on which most jokes are based.

£1.95 ☐

Yeuuch!
PETE SAUNDERS

A collection of revolting, horrible and disgusting things you'll wish you'd never discovered that will appeal to those who delight in gruesome detail. All the facts are true and many are highlighted by clever, zany illustrations.

£1.95 ☐

ARMADA

All these books are available at your local bookshop or newsagent, or can be ordered from the publisher. To order direct from the publishers just tick the title you want and fill in the form below:

Name _____

Address _____

_____

Send to: Collins Childrens Cash Sales
           PO Box 11
           Falmouth
           Cornwall
           TR10 9EN

Please enclose a cheque or postal order or debit my Visa/ Access –

   Credit card no:

   Expiry date:

   Signature:

– to the value of the cover price plus:

UK: 60p for the first book, 25p for the second book, plus 15p per copy for each additional book ordered to a maximum charge of £1.90.

BFPO: 60p for the first book, 25p for the second book plus 15p per copy for the next 7 books, thereafter 9p per book.

Overseas and Eire: £1.25 for the first book, 75p for the second book. Thereafter 28p per book.

Armada reserve the right to show new retail prices on covers which may differ from those previously advertised in the text or elswhere.

ARMADA